Gentle and Friendly Sea Lions

by Alice Collins

 HOUGHTON MIFFLIN HARCOURT
School Publishers

PHOTOGRAPHY CREDITS: Cover, ©Christian Science Monitor/Getty Images; p.3, ©Andre Jenny/Alamy; p.4, ©blickwinkel/Alamy; p5 ©John Francis/CORBIS; p.6 ©mastix/Alamy; p7, ©John Foxx Images/Dynamic Images/Jupiter; p.8, ©James Marshall/CORBIS; p.9, ©Andre Jenny/Alamy; p.10, ©DAVID GRAY/Reuters/Corbis; p.11, ©imagebroker / Alamy; p.12, ©Rudi Von Briel/PhotoEdit; p.14, ©CORBIS.

Printed in China

ISBN-10: 0-547-25314-1
ISBN-13: 978-0-547-25314-5

1 2 3 4 5 6 7 8 0940 18 17 16 15 14 13 12 11 10

Imagine an animal that can jump high out of the water. Imagine seeing long whiskers, or hairs, on this animal's face. Now imagine this marine mammal balancing a large ball on the tip of its nose. This animal lives mainly in the water. This animal is the sea lion, which is one of the most talented and intelligent creatures on earth.

Sea lion feeding time at an aquarium.

Sea lions

Sea lions often climb out of the water onto a beach.

Sea lions are *pinnipeds*, which means that they have fins instead of feet. Many different kinds of pinnipeds, including sea lions, walruses, and different types of seals, live in the oceans and in captivity, which means with humans. Sea lions are often trained to perform in shows at aquariums, which are large parks where people go to look at fish and sea mammals. The skin of sea lions is usually dark gray. They have long whiskers underneath their nose, and instead of feet, they have flippers. Most male sea lions weigh about 600 pounds (272 kg). Female sea lions are smaller, usually weighing only about 200 pounds (90.7 kg).

During mating season, male sea lions become very active. They try to defend the land near them. They also want to attract female sea lions. The largest sea lions usually have the best chances of mating. Because of this, male sea lions gain about 200 pounds (90.7 kg) in the weeks leading up to the mating time. Afterward, in what is called the molting season, male sea lions will lose all the weight they gained. They become very lazy and bask in the sun on the rocks as if they are stunned. They don't have much of an appetite, so they lose weight very quickly.

Male sea lions get angry during mating season.

Sea lions like to sit in the sun.

Sea lions that live on their own in the oceans usually live for about twenty years. However, when they are kept by people in an aquarium, sea lions can live more than thirty years. Sea lions are more likely to survive when they live with people who make certain that they get enough food and medical treatment. People with special training can detect and treat many problems a sea lion might have. Because of this, aquariums help sea lions.

Guthrie and Ballou are the names of two sea lions that live in an aquarium. They are both males. Guthrie is twenty-three years old, and his skin is a very dark color. Guthrie is very heavy for an adult male sea lion. During the mating time, Guthrie can weigh more than 900 pounds (408 kg)! He has long marks on his body where his skin has stretched from gaining so much weight.

Ballou is a much smaller sea lion who has lived with people in an aquarium since he was born. Ballou is sixteen years old, but he weighs only 350 pounds (159 kg). That is very small for an adult male. When Guthrie and Ballou swim together, you can see the difference in their sizes. Guthrie is more aggressive, or angry, and Ballou is more passive, or peaceful. This might be because Guthrie is so much bigger than Ballou.

Sea lions are cute!

You might think that you eat a lot, but you eat much less than a sea lion eats. Guthrie and Ballou eat a great many fish every day. Ballou usually eats 14.5 pounds (6.58 kg) of fish every day, an amount that contains 7,254 calories. A calorie is a measurement of energy. Guthrie eats even more. In one day, Guthrie can eat 39 pounds (17.7 kg) of fish, an amount that contains 20,816 calories! That is about how much food an adult person will eat in ten days.

Many people work in aquariums caring for sea lions.

Trainer

A trainer feeds two sea lions.

Just like people, sea lions like to eat different things. Guthrie and Ballou like to eat different types of fish, including herring and capelin. Sometimes they like one type of fish more than another kind.

The sea lions learn something each time they are fed in the aquarium. Each feeding is also an intensive teaching lesson. When sea lions are fed fish, they are taught to do different tricks. Their medicine is also placed in the fish they eat. Animal doctors called veterinarians are constantly analyzing the health of Guthrie and Ballou.

People also brush each sea lion's teeth so that a harmful substance called plaque will not appear on the teeth. This is very important because sea lions can get diseases of the mouth just like humans can if they don't have clean teeth and gums. Sea lions that live alone in the oceans don't need to have their teeth brushed because they catch their own fish to eat. When this happens, the fish move inside the sea lion's mouth, which rubs the plaque off of a sea lion's teeth.

Toothbrush

A sea lion gets its teeth brushed.

A sea lion swims underwater in an aquarium.

Each day, Guthrie and Ballou perform tricks for people who are visiting the aquarium. They do things like roll over, wave their flippers, and even bow to the audience. They have a great friendship with each other and with the people who train them. They are always very obedient in their calling as performers. Even if they are tired or not hungry, they know that the show must go on although it can sometimes be an ordeal!

These two sea lions have had the opportunity to learn some amazing things. For example, Guthrie can play tic-tac-toe, which is a game that people play.

On the walls outside the area where Guthrie and Ballou live, you can find pictures that were actually painted by these amazing sea lions. You probably make paintings in art class. The only difference between the paintings you make and the paintings made by Guthrie and Ballou is that Guthrie and Ballou's paintings were created using flippers instead of hands. With help from the people who train them, Guthrie and Ballou have learned how to paint and make beautiful designs.

Sea lions in aquariums perform many tricks for visitors.

People have taught Guthrie and Ballou many tricks. For example, if you hold out your hand with the thumb pointing up, the sea lions will stick their tongues out at you. If you wave to them when they are on land, they will wave to you by moving one of their flippers. Guthrie and Ballou really like it when people get very close to them. If you put your face close to one of the sea lions, he will kiss you. You can even stand behind them and pet their skin while they lay on the ground and make happy noises.

Sea lions haven't always been so lucky, however. Juvenile and adult sea lions were heavily hunted in the eighteenth and nineteenth centuries with fatal results. Several pinniped species, such as the Caribbean monk seal, became extinct, which means that all of them are dead.

The International Fur Seal Treaty of 1911 finally protected pinnipeds from people who hunt. However, many pinniped species remain at risk of becoming extinct. If we don't become more active in protecting these wonderful animals, we may lose them all.

Baby sea lions need to be protected

Baby sea lion

Responding

Cause and Effect What makes sea lions willing and able to perform tricks? Copy and complete the chart below.

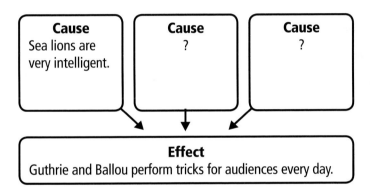

Cause
Sea lions are very intelligent.

Cause
?

Cause
?

Effect
Guthrie and Ballou perform tricks for audiences every day.

Write About It

Text to Text Write a paragraph about a different intelligent animal that you have read about in another book. Include details about how that animal behaves and the effects of that behavior.

✔ **TARGET VOCABULARY**

analyzing	juvenile
basking	marine
calling	ordeal
fatal	stunned
intensive	treating

✔ **TARGET SKILL** **Cause and Effect** Tell how events are related and how one event causes another.

✔ **TARGET STRATEGY** **Question** Ask questions about a selection before you read, as you read, and after you read.

GENRE **Informational Text** gives facts and examples about a topic.